The Dynamics of Personal Growth

Essential Skills for Transformation

Table of Contents

The only person you are destined to become is the person you decide to be.

Chapter 1. Introduction

Uncover hidden potential and step into a more fulfilled version of yourself with our latest Special Report: "The Dynamics of Personal Growth: Essential Skills for Transformation." Delve into an invigorating exploration of the internal mechanisms that power personal development and change. This engaging and enlightening report distills years of research into a comprehensive, yet digestible, roadmap for cultivating substantial self-improvement and leading a more fulfilling life. Empower your self-awareness, stoke your self-discovery, and inspire transformation that resonates from the core of your being. Find not just the motivation, but the practical skills necessary to make your growth dreams a reality. Now's the perfect time to embark on this vibrant journey of self-realization, because you, too, truly have the capacity to transform. Grab this special report — your passport to a better you — today!

Chapter 2. Understanding the Concept of Personal Growth

Personal growth... A term you've likely heard a myriad of times, spread across self-help books, motivational talks, and life coaching seminars alike. Yet, have we ever paused to ponder what this term truly encapsulates? Let's begin by diving deep into the underlying facets of personal growth, which is in essence an endless journey of self-discovery and self-evolution.

2.1. Understanding the Basics

Personal growth refers to the process of self-improvement, often through enhancing physical, mental, emotional, social and spiritual capacities. It is grounded in the belief that an individual can exploit their latent capabilities, effectively promoting an increased level of consciousness about oneself and their interactions with the world. Embarking on this path has the potential to enrich one's life in several ways, contributing to higher self-esteem, fulfilling relationships, professional success, and overall happiness and contentment.

A key point to note is that personal growth diverges from societal norms of success. Instead, it is much more introspective and individual-centric. It's not about accumulating wealth or achieving a specific job title, but about developing your authentic self and becoming the best version of who you truly are. Thus, personal growth is intrinsically based on self-awareness, identification and acceptance of one's strengths and weaknesses, and the courage to make necessary changes.

2.2. The Two Domains of Personal Growth

Personal growth exists in two distinct domains – the internal and the external.

Internal growth is about nurturing your spirit, identifying personal values, learning to handle emotions and gaining a sense of inner peace. It involves developing qualities such as resilience, adaptability, empathy, optimism, and commitment. This internal growth often leads to emotional maturation, spiritual enlightenment, and mental strengthening.

On the other hand, **external growth** encompasses developing skills, attributes, and competencies that enable you to interact more effectively with the world around you. This extends to acquiring intellectual and physical skills, enhancing communication abilities, and improving social and emotional relationships.

Ultimately, both domains are profoundly interconnected. Internal growth frequently prompts changes in external behavior, while external experiences can stimulate internal evolution.

2.3. The Stages of Personal Growth

Personal growth is not a one-off event. Instead, it's a transformative process that occurs over time, usually encompassing four distinct stages:

1. Unconscious Incompetence: You don't know that you don't know. We all begin our journey here, blissfully unaware of our ignorance or incompetence.

2. Conscious Incompetence: You know that you don't know. In this stage, you've recognized your incompetence and the need to

learn and grow.

3. Conscious Competence: You know that you know. Here, you begin to consciously practice until you've gained enough skill to do the tasked activity.

4. Unconscious Competence: You don't know that you know. This stage embodies mastery, wherein your skill is so deeply ingrained that it feels instinctual or automatic.

These stages form the backbone of personal growth, reminding us that gaining mastery takes effort, awareness, and time, and it doesn't stop there because there's always room to grow.

2.4. The Role of Self-Awareness

Personal growth starts with self-awareness. This is the ability to introspect and recognize one's thoughts, emotions, and behaviors, coupled with a deep understanding of one's strengths, weaknesses, and potential. Self-awareness shrinks the gap between our real self and our ideal self, becoming the driving force to guide us towards growth and transformation.

The key to developing self-awareness is honest self-reflection. By challenging your thoughts and questioning your beliefs, you can gain a deeper insight into your authentic self. This self-knowledge can empower you to make choices that align with your core values and augment personal growth.

2.5. The Mindset for Growth

Last but certainly not least, personal growth demands a certain mindset – a growth mindset. Championed by psychologist Carol Dweck, this concept suggests that our intellect and talents are not fixed traits, but can be developed over time with effort, perseverance, and resilience.

Individuals who foster a growth mindset perceive challenges as opportunities for growth and believe that their potential can be unlocked through continuous learning. They are not deterred by failure, instead viewing it as a stepping stone on the road to self-improvement.

In conclusion, understanding personal growth isn't just about knowing its stages or the factors that drive it. It is about recognizing it as a continuous journey of self-improvement and cultivation of the mind, emotions, and spirit – a holistic approach to becoming a better version of yourself. This journey may be long and arduous, marked by triumphs and failures, but it is ultimately worth it - a critically essential endeavor to living a fulfilling and meaningful life.

Chapter 3. The Importance of Self-Awareness in Personal Development

Engaging in an exploration of the significance of self-awareness in personal development compels us to recognize its invaluable role as the anchor, the beacon of light guiding us through our transformative journey. It implores us to ask, is self-awareness simply about recognizing our thoughts, feelings, and behaviors? Or is it about developing a critical understanding of our more profound nature, desires, purposes, beliefs, and values? The reality is, self-awareness is an amalgamation of all these facets, offering us a remarkable tool essential for personal growth and transformation.

3.1. The Spectrum of Self-Awareness

The journey of self-awareness begins with a comprehension of its broad spectrum. Remember, self-awareness is multi-faceted, extending from surface-level cognition to deeply introspective reflection. At the basic level, it involves understanding one's thoughts, emotions, and behaviors—the immediate cognitive and emotional responses to situations. A deeper level of self-awareness, however, involves recognizing one's inherent tendencies, ingrained beliefs, and longstanding values that shape our identity and define how we perceive and interact with the world. This spectrum of self-awareness is linked intricately with personal development, and grasping the entire spectrum is crucial to meaningful growth.

3.2. A Closer Look at Internal and External Self-Awareness

To understand self-awareness more deeply, let's compartmentalize it into 'internal' and 'external' self-awareness. Internal self-awareness refers to understanding one's internal states, preferences, resources, and intuitions. It's about attuning to your deeper ambitions, beliefs, strengths, and weaknesses. Conversely, external self-awareness pertains to comprehending how others perceive us, which is often a mirror to our blind spots. A harmonious blend of these two types can lead to a profound comprehension of oneself and our impact on others, fueling meaningful personal transformation.

3.3. Implications of Self-Awareness for Personal Development

Indeed, self-awareness wields enormous implications for personal development. It fosters emotional intelligence, equipping us to navigate complex human emotions skillfully. By understanding our triggers, we can respond more mindfully, defusing conflicts and cementing relationships. Self-awareness also paves the way for empathy, enabling us to appreciate different perspectives, thereby promoting tolerance, open-mindedness, and compassion. It imparts a greater sense of purpose and direction in life, influencing our decision-making and goal-setting processes. By unearthing our authentic selves, it emboldens us to make choices that align with our core values, facilitating fulfillment and satisfaction.

Furthermore, self-awareness forms the bedrock of change. Awakening to our current state is the first step towards growth, highlighting areas for development and potential hurdles. It enables us to measure our progress and maintain our growth trajectory. In essence, self-awareness shapes our journey from where we stand presently, to where we aspire to be.

3.4. The Paradox of Introspection

While self-awareness is coveted, it's not always guaranteed by introspection. This seeming paradox emerges because introspection often revolves around asking 'why.' Delving into why we feel a certain way or why we act in a particular manner can lead us astray, reinforcing existing beliefs and biases instead of challenging them. Instead, shift the lens from 'why' to 'what.' What are my current emotions? What am I planning to do next? This approach breeds clarity, enabling us to remain anchored in our current experience and encouraging constructive self-examination.

3.5. Cultivating Self-Awareness: Practical Strategies

Embracing self-awareness involves practical strategies that usher self-discovery and growth. Mindfulness and meditation are potent tools for nurturing internal self-awareness, encouraging us to tune into our thoughts, emotions, and body sensations without judgment. Self-reflection through journaling can also yield significant insights into our inner self. Involving trusted others can cultivate external self-awareness, as their objective viewpoints can reveal blind spots in our self-perception.

Self-awareness takes time, patience, and perseverance, but the rewards in personal development are immense. It forms the crux of our transformation, empowering us to forge our path towards fulfillment with greater clarity, purpose, and authenticity. Hold the mirror of self-awareness close—an enlightened version of yourself awaits discovery.

In conclusion, self-awareness serves not just as the cornerstone of personal development, but as the compass directing us towards a more profound understanding of ourselves and the world around us.

It unfolds a journey of exploration from the surface realities of our behaviors and feelings to the deepest corners of our desires and values. This journey beckons us all—invitations to understand, grow, and transform into a better version of ourselves.

Chapter 4. Unlocking Your Potential: Strategies for Effective Self-Reflection

Central to your personal development journey is the commitment to unlock your potential—a hidden reservoir of ability that, when tapped into, can drastically alter the trajectory of your life and overall well-being. Self-reflection is one of the key strategies to achieving this. Please note this is not an overnight transformation but rather a process demanding both patience and persistence. Nonetheless, the fortitude to engage in regular self-reflection will lay the groundwork for a transformative experience.

4.1. The Significance of Self-Reflection

Self-reflection stands as a potent method of understanding the essence of your being, the mechanics of your mind, and the result of your decisions. It imparts a crucial understanding of your strengths and weaknesses, beliefs, fears, desires, and a variety of other essential aspects integral to personal development and attainment of a fulfilling life.

The journey of self-reflection is much like an open conversation with oneself - where you, the self, and the universe align. It's a point of intersection between what is known, unknown, and what spans beyond comprehension. It constitutes an inner dialogue that weaves the narrative of your existence and lends meaning to every thought, action, and emotion.

4.2. Setting the Stage for Self-Reflection

To unlock the potential within, it's essential to transform your self-reflective escapades into regular practice. Developing an individualized self-reflection routine that comfortably fits into your lifestyle can propel your personal growth exponentially.

Creating an enabling environment is a fundamental starting point. This can be a quiet room free of distractions, the solitude of dawn, or the ambiance of lit candles with soft music—whatever fuels concentration, sparks introspection, and beckons a peaceful state of mind. Support your environment with a comfortable seating position and a conducive time slot that accommodates unhurried, unrushed reflection.

Incorporate it into your daily routine, like brushing your teeth or eating breakfast. This consistency helps form habits, and regular self-reflection will eventually become an indispensable part of your day.

Devices like schedulers, timers, wearable tech, and productivity apps can be a big help in reminding and measuring your commitment to self-reflection. Also, traditional tools like journals or diaries can be utilized for recording thoughts and reflecting on experiences.

4.3. The Art of Questioning

The art of questioning is pivotal in self-reflection. Questioning uncovers critical insights, clears ambiguity, and reveals authenticity. A few core questions to consider might include:

- What have I learned today?

- How have my actions aligned with my values?

- What could I have done differently?

- Where do I see myself in the near future based on my current trajectory?

These questions drive deeper thinking and unmask the unknown, giving you strength and wisdom to propel positive transformations in your personal growth journey.

4.4. Navigating Self-Criticism

An essential aspect of self-reflection involves cultivating your abilities to self-analyze and self-criticize. However, it's paramount to approach self-criticism constructively, using it as a tool for nurturing positive change rather than breeding negative self-perception.

Constructive self-criticism focuses on recognizing flaws without judgment and presents an opportunity to learn and improve. It's about understanding your shortcomings, not to berate, but to identify areas for improvement. This empowers you with the necessary insight to break away from detrimental habits, fostering personal growth and unlocking potential.

4.5. The Role of Emotional Intelligence

Emotional intelligence plays a crucial role in effective self-reflection. Understanding and managing your emotions, empathizing with others, and maintaining successful relationships are central to emotional intelligence—all of which enable deeper self-reflection.

Developing emotional intelligence includes gaining a sense of self-awareness—recognizing your emotions as they occur. Self-reflection is a powerful tool here, with the potential to deepen your understanding of emotional responses and attitudes, thereby guiding personal growth and positive change.

4.6. Leveraging Self-Reflection for Proactive Change

Analyze your self-reflection findings to augment your life proactively. Through the insights gleaned from self-reflection, visualize a future that realigns with your core values, reallocate energy to meaningful pursuits, and reshape your behavior to better suit your growth goals. Above all, allow the course of self-reflection to steer you towards the path of self-acceptance and personal fulfillment.

In conclusion, the journey of personal growth, despite its challenges, is an adventurous path filled with opportunities for profound learning and self-discovery. Implementing effective self-reflection builds the bridge spanning from your present self to the improved future version you envision. The first step starts with you—ready to unlock your potential and embrace the exciting, fulfilling journey that awaits!

Chapter 5. The Role of Emotions in Personal Growth

The journey of personal growth is inextricably linked to our emotional landscape, a vital yet often underestimated component that underpins our capacity for change, resilience, and self-realization. It is through understanding and mastering our emotions that we begin to truly harness our potential. This chapter embarks on a comprehensive exploration of the significant role emotions play in personal growth.

5.1. Understanding Emotion as a Part of Human Complexity

Emotions are an inherent part of our human complexity. They serve as indicators, signposts that guide us to understand our subjective experience of reality. Whether it's joy, sadness, fear, or anger, every emotion we feel provides a glimpse into our internal state, influencing our perceptions, decisions, and actions. By learning to understand and manage our emotions, we can steer our personal growth in meaningful ways and nurture healthier relationships with ourselves and others.

Daniel Goleman's seminal work on Emotional Intelligence (EQ) underscores the idea that our emotions, far from being peripheral to our growth, are central to it. Contrary to an age-old assumption that rationality reigns supreme, Goleman posits that emotional intelligence – the ability to understand and manage our emotions and the emotions of others – is a significant determinant of success and fulfillment in life.

5.2. The Interplay of Emotions and Personal Growth

Understanding the intricate interplay between emotions and personal growth requires recognition of how emotions function. They result from individual appraisal processes that reflect our evaluations and interpretations of our experiences.

Here are the critical ways emotions intersect with personal growth:

- Emotions as Catalysts for Growth: Powerful emotions, positive or negative, can be catalysts for growth by pushing us out of our comfort zones, prompting introspection and a re-evaluation of our goals and values.

- Emotions as Navigational Tools: Emotions can act as navigational tools, guiding us in personal decision-making. Paying attention to our emotional responses can provide us with valuable insights into our needs, preferences, and areas of discontent.

- Emotions as Bridges for Empathy: Emotions can foster a deeper connection with others, facilitating empathetic relationships. Empathy plays a crucial role in our social growth as relational beings, underscoring our interconnectedness, and enhancing our collective growth.

5.3. Unpacking Emotional Intelligence

Emotional Intelligence is, as John D. Mayer and Peter Salovey described, the ability to perceive emotions, to access and generate emotions so as to assist thought, to understand emotions and emotional knowledge and to regulate emotions to promote emotional and intellectual growth. There are four primary components of emotional intelligence, which we will now delve into with more detail.

1. Self-Awareness: This refers to the ability to recognize and understand our own emotions, discriminate between different feeling states, and acknowledge their impact on our behavior and thoughts.

2. Self-Management: This involves the capacity to regulate our emotions, manage stress, practice delayed gratification, and create an environment conducive for productivity and wellbeing.

3. Social Awareness: This dimension involves empathy, the ability to understand the emotions, needs, and concerns of others, and to recognize emotional cues and dynamics in social situations.

4. Relationship Management: This incorporates skills like communication, conflict management, and the building and nurturing of positive relationships.

By developing and enhancing these components of emotional intelligence, we can effectively harness our emotions to facilitate personal growth.

5.4. Guiding Emotions, Directing Personal Growth

So how does one wield the dynamics of these emotional components towards personal growth? Here's a structured roadmap for you.

1. Identifying Emotions: Start by being mindful of your emotional state. Practice naming your emotions as you experience them. This practice isn't about self-judgment or criticism but is a step to understand oneself better.

2. Feelings as Data: Treat your feelings as data points. They are signals about your beliefs, values, expectations, or perceived threats.

3. Emotion Regulation: Once you have identified and understood your emotions, work towards managing them. Learn and practice techniques such as mindfulness, cognitive reframing, and relaxation exercises to better regulate your emotional responses.

4. Responsive, not Reactive: Using emotions as data and learning to regulate them helps you become responsive rather than reactive, leading to better decision-making under stress.

5. Empathizing with Others: Remember, empathy extends your emotional understanding to others, making for richer, deeper connections and social growth.

6. Seeking Professional Help: If regulating emotions becomes overwhelming, don't hesitate to seek professional help. Therapists and counselors are equipped to support you in your journey towards emotional intelligence and personal growth.

Mastering your emotions, while challenging, is a continuing endeavor. It involves facing discomfort, making wise choices, and cultivating empathy for oneself and others. This journey, however, is vital to personal growth, painting a richer, more nuanced picture of ourselves. As we increasingly understand and artfully wield our emotions, we pave the path for transformation and step into a more fulfilled version of ourselves. So let your emotions serve not as hindrances, but as illuminating guides in your personal growth odyssey. And remember: it's beautiful to feel. For as Naomi Shihab Nye wrote in her evocative poem 'Kindness', 'Before you know kindness as the deepest thing inside, / you must know sorrow as the other deepest thing'.

Chapter 6. Bringing Change: Adopting a Growth Mindset

The world, notwithstanding its constant pace, is ever-evolving and changing. For individuals like you and me, this presents an opportunity to engage in profound personal development; a chance to adapt ourselves to better fit the dynamic world around us. This evolutionary process is propelled by what is referred to as a 'Growth Mindset.' Having a Growth Mindset prompts us to embrace challenges, persist in the face of setbacks, and see effort not as fruitless labor, but as the route to mastery.

6.1. Understanding the Growth Mindset

The concept of a Growth Mindset was first introduced by psychologist Carol Dweck, after years of research on achievement and success. Dweck observed that individuals can be broadly classified into two categories — those with a 'Fixed Mindset' who believe their abilities can't be changed, and those with a 'Growth Mindset,' who understand that their talents and skills can be bolstered with effort, learning, and persistence.

Individuals with a Growth Mindset tend to rise higher in their personal and professional lives as they believe they can develop their abilities, steering them towards a path of continuous learning and resilience in the face of setbacks. They accept that they might not be good at something initially, but also recognize that they can improve with time and effort. They comprehend that intelligence and talent are merely starting points that can be further honed and are not fixed entities.

6.2. Shifting from Fixed to Growth Mindset

Understanding the concept of Fixed and Growth Mindsets is not enough; the true power lies in implementing the Growth Mindset in daily life. Although the first step lies in recognizing the concept, the real journey begins with practice and application. The trick is to exchange the Fixed Mindset with a Growth Mindset by consciously changing how one perceives abilities and potential, an exercise that requires diligence and effort.

Whenever you find yourself thinking 'I am not good at this,' shift your thinking to 'I am not good at this, yet.' This subtle change in phrasing encapsulates the essence of the Growth Mindset: learning is a process, and room for improvement always exists. You can improve your mindset by embracing challenges, being persistent in the face of adversity, learning from criticism, and finding lessons and inspiration in the success of others. Over time, such practices will help transform your mindset, leading to a richer, more productive personal and professional life.

6.3. The Robustness of the Growth Mindset in Overcoming Challenges

The Growth Mindset possesses a stupendous potential for fostering resilience in individuals. It teaches us to view challenges not as insurmountable obstacles but opportunities for learning and growth. The key lies in shifting our perception of failures: From marks of defeat to sources of learning, from heavy setbacks to stepping stones to improvement. This increased resilience not only helps in personal development but also assists in successfully traversing the bouts of uncertainties and difficulties that life invariably catapults our way.

6.4. The Spiral of Continuous Learning: Growth Mindset's Impetus

Individuals with a Growth Mindset realize that no skill or information is ever wasted. They have an inherent understanding that even seemingly unrelated skills or knowledge can serve to improve their overall competency and potential. This perspective makes them lifelong learners, forever seeking new information, skills, and experiences. By constantly stepping outside their comfort zones and into the unknown, they ensure that they continue to learn, grow, and evolve.

In conclusion, cultivating a Growth Mindset proves indispensable for navigating the constantly-evolving world around us. It helps one rise to challenges and view them as roads to success rather than impediments. It fosters resilience, motivates learning, and encourages self-improvement. So, remember, the roadblocks you face today are not the end of your journey; they're merely rests, teaching important lessons for navigating the future path. Tirelessly cultivate a Growth Mindset, and the path to personal growth will unfurl before you, full of vibrant opportunities.

Chapter 7. The Power of Positive Affirmations and Visualization

The mechanism behind affirmations and visualization is deeply rooted in the psychology of human behavior and cognition. These two powerful tools play pivotal roles in the human mind's capacity for self-change and personal growth. Harnessing the power of positive affirmations and visualization can unlock an untapped vault of potential inside you, catapulting you to new heights in your personal development journey. Let's delve into an in-depth exploration of these two transformative strategies.

7.1. Understanding Positive Affirmations

Positive affirmations are concise, positive statements targeted at a specific subconscious set of beliefs, to challenge and undermine negative beliefs and replace them with positive self-nurturing beliefs. They are not merely feel-good catchphrases, and their effectiveness lies in their regular repetition and emotional charge. Used correctly, they serve to reprogram our mental patterns, replacing negative thought process with more constructive ones, ultimately culminating in a shift in perception and behavior.

Skepticism might arise given the simplicity of the concept, but a myriad of research supports the potency of positive affirmations. Psychologists and neuroscientists have showcased how constant repetition of positive affirmations leads to changes in neural connectivity, essentially rewiring the brain.

7.2. The Influence of Visualization

Positive affirmations, while powerful on their own, can be supplemented with a related technique - visualization - to amplify their impact. Visualization pertains to the practice of creating a mental image or intention of your desired outcomes. It can pertain to anything from picturing yourself acing a job interview, to envisioning being in a state of zen-like calm in a stressful situation.

Visualization operates under the premise that 'seeing is believing', and since your brain can often struggle to differentiate between what is real and what is imagined, presenting it with vivid, positive mental imagery trains it into manifesting those outcomes in reality. This technique is widely used in a variety of areas from sports psychology to cognitive behavioural therapy and has received empirical support in the form of neuroimaging studies showcasing that mental practices can enhance motivation, increase confidence, and improve motor performance.

7.3. The Symbiosis Between Positive Affirmations and Visualization

Positive affirmations and visualization have individual strengths but used in tandem, they forge a symbiosis that creates an even more potent tool for personal development. As you feed your mind with positive affirmations, your beliefs start shifting, and as this shift happens, visualization paints the mental imagery that lends credence to those new beliefs. The more vivid the imagery generated via visualization, the greater the belief in the possibility of the affirmed reality.

7.4. Implementation Techniques: Affirmations and Visualization in Practice

To harness the power of these techniques, it's crucial to integrate them into your everyday routine. For affirmations, make sure they are positive, brief, in the present tense, and targeted towards a specific goal or area in your life. Repeat them multiple times a day - when you wake up, during downtime like daily commutes, and just before you go to bed. Utilize creative techniques like writing them down or singing them out loud to enhance their impression.

Visualization exercises work best when in a relaxed state. Dedicating specific time daily, even just a few minutes, to close your eyes and create vivid images of your goals enhances the impact. Adding details - sights, sounds, smells, feelings - makes the visualization feel more real to the brain, and therefore, more likely to be believed and acted upon.

7.5. Cautionary Note: Pitfalls to Avoid

While the benefits are monumental, there are pitfalls to avoid in using affirmations and visualization. aiming too high with your affirmations can lead to disillusionment, as unrealistically high expectations go unmet. Keep affirmations realistic and progressive. Similarly, with visualization, it's important not to swing into the zone of daydreaming. You're not merely creating a fantasy, but setting an intention for reality.

Personal growth is an ongoing process, and incorporating the power of positive affirmations and visualization into your life is one significant way to foster this growth. While this chapter provides the tools, it's the consistent, committed action from you that truly spurs transformation. As you infuse positivity into your mindset and paint your aspirations on your mental canvas, you are well on your way to manifesting the desired changes in your life.

Chapter 8. Building Resilience: Navigating Life's Challenges

In the tapestry of personal growth, resilience occupies a significant area. It is the human ability to recover from setbacks, adapt to change, and keep going. Resilience doesn't merely serve as a protective barrier against life's hardships; it's the buoyant force that enables us to navigate them with grace, learning, healing, and growth.

8.1. The Power of Resilience

Resilience is an extraordinary power that every individual possesses, although its strength varies among us. It lies dormant within the psyche, ready to surge forward in times of crisis. For some, this might be a natural reflex; for others, a skill that requires cultivation. The fact remains that resilience is inherently versatile — a survival instinct honed by evolution and a psychological tool we can learn to wield more effectively.

8.2. Understanding the Mechanisms of Resilience

Investigating the constituents of resilience provides us with the blueprint to enhance it. Resilience stems from several interlinked components:

1. Emotional Intelligence - Enables us to recognize, understand, and manage our emotions, along with those of others.

2. Problem-Solving Skills - Equip us to analyze and address

difficulties rather than avoid them.

3. Social Connections - Foster a sense of belonging and emotional support, an external form of resilience.

4. Wellness Practices - Aid in maintaining physical, mental, and emotional well-being, fortifying overall resilience.

Each component represents a gear which, when synergized with others, forms a robust resilience engine. Investing in each aspect equips us to adeptly navigate life's challenges.

8.3. Developing Emotional Intelligence

Emotional intelligence, or EI, serves as the emotional compass guiding us through our journey. Enhancing EI involves the following steps:

1. Implement regular 'emotional check-ins' - Identify and label your emotions, accepting them without judgment.

2. Practice mindfulness - This allows staying present in the moment and observing feelings from a distance, preventing being swept away by a tempest of emotions.

3. Foster empathy - Strive to understand others' emotional experiences, leading to deeper, more supportive relationships.

8.4. Building Effective Problem-Solving Skills

The ability to approach and solve problems proactively is another cornerstone of resilience.

1. Brainstorm solutions - Adopt a growth mindset allowing you to

view obstacles as opportunities for learning.

2. Logical thinking - Apply logic and reason in evaluating your options, rather than making decisions dominated by emotions.

3. Try, try again - Persistence is an integral part of the process. Even unsuccessful attempts yield invaluable learning opportunities.

8.5. Cultivating Social Connections

Healthy social connections constitute an exterior scaffold bolstering our resilience in trying times.

1. Be present - Engage more genuinely in interactions. Steer away from digital distractions and give your undivided attention.

2. Invest in relationships - Cultivating relationships is akin to planting seeds and tending to them to produce a healthy, robust plant.

3. Seek support - Allow yourself to lean on loved ones during tough times; it's a testament to strength, not a giveaway of weakness.

8.6. Embracing Wellness Practices

A healthy body and mind serve as the unwavering platform upon which resilience rests.

1. Regular movement - Exercise releases endorphins, improves mood, boosts self-esteem, and alleviates stress.

2. Balanced nutrition - A nutrient-rich diet fuels the body and brain, enhancing your ability to cope.

3. Sleep hygiene - Quality sleep restores both body and mind, increasing your capacity to handle stress.

4. Mind-body practices like meditation, yoga, or Tai Chi can cultivate calmness and equanimity, promoting resilience.

8.7. Embedding Resilience into Daily Life

Having understood and embarked on cultivating resilience, it is critical to embed it into our everyday lives. This involves artful execution of the previously discussed skills, a commitment to practice them daily, and the continued pursuit of self-improvement. Through this, we transcend from merely weathering life's storms to skillfully surfing through them, leading to a more fulfilled life.

In conclusion, building resilience is transformative — it helps us effectively navigate challenges, extract lessons and growth opportunities from them, and emerge stronger. It can be a complex process but remember: we do not simply build resilience in grand, defining moments, but also in the mundane ticks of everyday existence. This engagement with resilience not only instigates transformation but fosters the capacity to uphold it, leading us into a more fulfilled version of ourselves.

Chapter 9. Improving Interpersonal Skills for Holistic Growth

Even as we delve into the very core of personal enrichment, it's impossible to circumvent the topic of interpersonal skills, particularly given their pivotal role in holistic metamorphosis. These social abilities — or our capacity for creating and maintaining healthy relationships with others — serve as the vital cog in our personal and professional lives. Not only are these skills essential in sustaining lifelong friendships, but they also form the robust foundation upon which we construct our careers, partnerships, and ultimately, our life trajectories.

9.1. The Essence of Interpersonal Skills

Interpersonal skills encapsulate our capacity to interact effectively with others. They encompass communication prowess, emotional intelligence, empathy, and the ability to mediate and negotiate situations. Collectively, these skills shape how we perceive and respond to those around us, and, indubitably they largely determine our experiences and satisfaction with our social sphere.

Multiple studies have illustrated the substantial influence these interpersonal capabilities have on multiple facets of our lives. Notably, they're found to substantially impact our overall happiness and wellbeing, career progression, and the quality of our relationships. Therefore, a mindful cultivation of these competencies is more than just a desirable pursuit; it's an essential undertaking for a balanced and productive life.

9.2. The Art of Communication

Undeniably, communication is the cornerstone of effective interpersonal exchange. Mastery of both verbal and non-verbal means of communication, from language and tone modulation to body language and facial expression, is an integral cog in this complex wheel.

Expressing oneself with clarity propels understanding, facilitates efficient problem-solving, and inspires collaboration. Moreover, by adapting your communication style to the listener's needs, empathy and understanding can be invoked, considerably enhancing the efficacy of your interactions.

Observe the nuances of your conversation partner's speech and body language: are they at ease? Is their posture suggesting they're receptive to your input, or do they exhibit signs of disinterest or annoyance? Understanding these subtleties will help you enormously in steering the conversation's direction and effectively engaging with the person on the other end.

9.3. Emotional Intelligence and Empathy

Emotional intelligence heralds our ability to acknowledge, comprehend, and manage not just our own emotions, but those of others we interact with. It's the foundation for empathy, and a high degree of it can drastically enhance the quality of our interpersonal relationships.

Exhibiting empathy — that is, the capacity to comprehend and share the feelings of others — is a profoundly human attribute, one that can embellish our interactions with warmth, understanding, and mutual respect. By taking the time to understand another's perspective, we foster rapport and build robust, enduring relationships.

9.4. Conflict Resolution: Mediation and Negotiation

In any social or professional setting, an occasional discord is inevitable. However, our ability to mediate such conflicts, standing as an unbiased intermediary, and negotiate resolutions that fulfill all parties involved, can dramatically improve the inter-relational dynamic within a group. An adept negotiator transcends barriers, smoothen miscommunication, and cultivates an atmosphere of peaceful cooperation.

Learn to balance your perspective with those of others. Practice listening with an open mind, refrain from interruptive judgment, and encourage free expression. Aim for solutions that satisfy the broader interests of all parties rather than rigidly sticking to preconceived notions.

9.5. Integrating It All: Strengthening Your Interpersonal Abilities

Improving these skills commands a multi-pronged approach. From engaging in active listening, assertive communication, aligning body language, to employing empathy and practicing conflict resolution — each plays a monumental role in this enriching journey.

By creating a conscious, concerted effort to cultivate these skills, we lay the groundwork for a well-rounded, vibrant life experience. Our interactions become more rewarding, our understanding of others deepens, and our tolerance for divergent views strengthens. This dovetails into diverse benefits: professional advancement, more fulfilling personal relationships, and an enriched sense of connection with the social fabric that we are part of.

This painstaking yet enriching process of improvement doesn't happen overnight. Changing habitual patterns of interaction demands patience, dedication, and consistency. However, with a steadfast commitment to refining these skills, you will be well positioned to unlock a more fulfilled, enriched version of yourself, replete with the capacity to forge and nurture beneficial relationships in all walks of life.

In a vying world that often prioritizes individual accomplishments, we must recognize that our ability to interact effectively, empathetically, and meaningfully with others is a keystone of success and happiness. So embark on refining your interpersonal skills — the rewards will be manifold and far-reaching. Embrace this path and you'll find that not only are you growing as an individual, but you are also uplifting others around you, fostering a fertile ground for collective edification.

Chapter 10. Nurturing a Life-long Learning Attitude: Embracing New Skills and Knowledge

The potent scent of curiosity and the zest for understanding, often associated with the heart of human adventure, isn't reserved for the youth; it's a quality we can cultivate and enjoy throughout our entire lives. One of the keys to sustainable transformation and personal growth is nurturing a life-long learning attitude, constantly looking for opportunities to embrace new skills and knowledge. This can be a challenging shift, requiring consistent effort, perseverance, and introspection. Our journey will explore the benefits of life-long learning, tips for developing an open mindset to new knowledge, and strategies for effectively cultivating and incorporating new skills into your daily life.

10.1. The Lifelong Learning Mindset

Life-long learning is a term used to express the continuous, self-motivated pursuit of knowledge for personal reasons or professional competence. The importance of a life-long learning mindset cannot be overstated in the context of personal growth. It is the spark that inspires us to explore the unexplored and to venture forth into new arenas of understanding. It encourages us to face the unknown with exuberance, replacing fear with curiosity.

Lifelong learning is more than absorbing information; it's about understanding how to learn and applying that skill to any area you are passionate about. It involves keeping an open mind, curiosity, conscientiousness, the ability to regulate our learning, and resilience in the face of challenges.

10.2. Embracing New Skills and Knowledge

Now that we understand the essence of a life-long learning mindset, how do we go about embracing new skills and knowledge effectively? The journey starts by acknowledging that everyone has their unique style and pace of learning. Understanding your preferred method of learning can significantly improve the effectiveness of your learning process. Whether you're a visual, auditory, reading/writing, or kinesthetic learner, adopting strategies that correspond with your learning style will amplify your ability to assimilate new information.

Next, it's crucial to cultivate the quality of 'wanting to learn.' By instilling in ourselves a genuine curiosity about the world around us, we open numerous avenues for learning, growth, and discovery. There's no shortage of material to delve into - articles, books, online courses, podcasts are just a few examples.

10.3. Applying Skills and Knowledge into Daily Life

Immersing yourself in new ideas and skills is only part of the journey towards personal growth. The true transformation occurs when we apply these learnings into our everyday life, refining and adapting them to suit our personal circumstances. Start with small, incremental changes. Can you apply your new learning to your relationships, your work, or your personal projects? With each application, you refine your understanding and make the learning truly yours.

Moreover, it's important to remember that learning isn't a linear process, and quite often involves revisiting previously acquired knowledge or skills. Remembering to revisit our learnings from time to time allows us to reflect, refocus, and ensure that we're truly embedding this new knowledge into our psyche.

10.4. Lifelong Learning: A Journey, Not a Destination

As humans, we are continually growing and expanding. The process of life-long learning echoes this truth. It's not about arriving at a final destination; instead, it's a journey, one that's paved with the joy of discovery, the exhilaration of new insights and fresh perspectives.

In conclusion, nurturing a life-long learning attitude is integral to embracing new skills and knowledge. It fuels personal growth, propels us out of our comfort zones, and encourages us to pursue a more informed, fulfilled, and dynamic existence. Remember, every new piece of information has the potential to add a new dimension to your worldview. So, stay curious, stay open, and never stop learning.

Chapter 11. Embedding Personal Growth into Everyday Life: A Sustainable Transformation

Contrary to popular belief, personal growth does not necessitate dramatic, life-altering changes or the pursuit of hefty and lofty goals in a condensed time period. A more constructive and long-lasting approach focuses on incorporating elements of personal growth into daily life, leading to subtle but significant transformations over time. By transforming personal growth into an integral part of your daily existence, you assure its sustainability, hence attempting to address the core theme of this chapter - 'Embedding Personal Growth into Everyday Life: A Sustainable Transformation.'

11.1. Embracing a Growth Mindset

One of the decisive first steps to embedding personal growth into your everyday life involves embracing a 'growth' mindset – a viewpoint that encourages learning, embraces challenges, and persists in the face of setbacks. This mindset postulates the belief that certain abilities can be developed and are not necessarily inherent. Nurturing a growth mindset transforms daily life into a fertile ground for learning and development. Be willing to make mistakes, take risks, and fail. Recognize these instances not as defeats, but as opportunities to learn and improve. Forge the habit of replacing negative thoughts with a growth-oriented perspective, steadily turning this adjustment into your regular mental framework.

11.2. The Art of Mindful Living

Cultivating mindfulness can greatly aid in integrating personal growth into your everyday life. To 'live mindfully' is to fully engage with the present moment. It entails immersing yourself completely into your current experience, paying careful attention to minute details and nuances, and ceding any preoccupation with the past or future. This way, even mundane tasks become vessels of growth. By washing dishes mindfully, for example, you not only cleanse the wares but also trim down stress, increase focus, and foster gratitude for clean water and food.

11.3. Making Time for Reflection

When integrating personal growth into daily life, carving out time for self-reflection should never be neglected. Nourishing this practice offers insights into your innermost thoughts, beliefs, and attitudes – illuminating strengths and spotlighting areas for improvement. Spend a few moments each day pondering and recording your feelings and experiences, perusing the patterns and themes that surface. This habit of reflection redirects your focus toward continual improvement and self-understanding.

11.4. Utilizing Affirmations and Visualization

Daily affirmations and visualizations can gradually transform your subconscious mind, moulding it to confide in your potential and execute changes. Vigorously repeat positive messages about yourself, your capabilities, and your goals daily. Visualize yourself as you aspire to be, successfully navigating various tasks and challenges. Regular practice of these exercises bolsters self-belief, driving you towards the fulfilling life you envision.

11.5. Adopting Lifelong Learning

Cultivating an attitude of life-long learning is a cornerstone of embedding personal growth into everyday life. This principle embodies consistent learning and an unquenchable thirst for knowledge. Despite the formality of educational institutions, genuine learning isn't restricted to structured environments. Read widely, enrol in online courses, listen to podcasts, engage in enlightening conversations; these are all avenues for everyday intellectual and personal growth.

11.6. Nurturing Relationships

Relationships offer fertile ground for personal development, providing opportunities for learning about emotional management, empathy, communication, and respect. Approaching relationships as a domain of growth promotes the honing of these skills, leading to enriched personal interactions and expanding personal growth in everyday life.

By embedding these principles and practices into your daily life, a sustainable avenue is carved out for personal growth that integrates seamlessly with your routine. The transformation experienced when personal growth becomes a lifestyle rather than a task is profound, leading to increased self-awareness, resilience, fulfilment, and the achievement of your potential. After all, it is such adaptations in everyday living that forges the path towards sustained positive transformation.